NEVER WEAR BLACK SOCKS OR A PLAIN WHITE T-SHIRT WHILE RUNNING

AND 501 OTHER TRUTHS TOO SIMPLE NOT TO KNOW

By

Joe Kelly

Illustrated By:

Anna Skramko Hosford

(P.T.L)

Good Times Publishing
Utica, NY

Good Times Publishing
PO Box 4545
Utica, NY 13504

Library of Congress Cataloging-in-Publication Data
Kelly, Joe, 1946-
Never wear a plain white t-shirt or black socks while running: And 501 other truths too simple not to know / Joe Kelly / Illustrated by Anna Skramko Hosford
p. cm.
ISBN 0-9639290-5-4
1. Running 2. Title.
GV1061.K45 1996
796.4'2--dc20

96-20134
CIP
Printed in Central New York

Also By Joe Kelly

Utica Sesquicentennial Scrapbook

Joe Kelly's Greatest Ever
Little Trivia Book

The Train Doesn't Stop In Wagner,
Montana Anymore
And Neither Do I
(Travels In America)

I've Been Writing A Newspaper Column For So Long
I Don't Think I Could Hold A Real Job Anymore
(The Wit & Wisdom of Joe Kelly)

ABOUT THE AUTHOR

Joe Kelly lives and works in Utica, New York, which is in the center of the state. When it comes to running, Utica is famous for two things: the Boilermaker Road Race and America's Greatest Heart Run & Walk.

Kelly is assistant race director of the Boilermaker, which Runner's World magazine has selected as one of the "top 65 races" in the country. He also helps organize America's Greatest Heart Run & Walk, which raises more than $500,000 every year for the American Heart Association.

Since 1982 he has written a weekly newspaper column about running for the (Utica) Observer-Dispatch. He is on the PRRO (Professional Road Running Organization) board of directors, carried the Olympic torch in the 1996 cross country relay and has run hundreds of races throughout the country, including five marathons. Once he even broke four hours at the New York City Marathon. The wind was at his back.

This book is dedicated to the more than 2,500 volunteers who make the Boilermaker Road Race such a success and to the thousands of cheering spectators who make running the Boilermaker such fun.

INTRODUCTION

There's nothing complicated about running. You put one foot in front of the other and try not to trip. But there are things to learn about running, truths too simple not to know.

The idea for this book came while I was teaching a class at Mohawk Valley Community College. The class was for runners wanting to participate in their first Boilermaker Road Race, a 15-K race which is run in Utica, NY on the second Sunday of every July. Because the race generates so much publicity, the field always has a high percentage of first time Boilermaker runners.

The students in these Boilermaker classes come in various

some are beginners. All, though, are enthusiastic about running.

The students have something else in common. All of them are looking for advice. They want tips they can take home from class and use in the race and wherever else their running takes them. So I went in search of an instruction book for runners.

There are many books about running, some are even great books. None of them, though, was the type of instruction book I was looking for, which is why I put together the one you are holding in your hands.

Joe Kelly,
Utica, NY

1. Set goals for your running.

2. Put your goals in writing.

3. Post your goals where you and others can see them.

4. Make this one of your goals: to run at least three miles in all 50 states.

5. Subscribe to as many running publications as you can afford.

6. Volunteer to work at races.

7. Read Dr. George Sheehan's "Running & Being."

8. Never wear headphones in a race.

9. Join your local running club.

10. If your community has no running club, start one.

11. Support friends who are training for a marathon.

12. Thank race workers for volunteering.

13. Own two good pair of running shoes. Rotate them.

14. Run facing traffic.

15. Never drop out of a race just because your finishing time is going to be slow.

16. Don't be embarrassed to drop out of a race if you have an injury or other medical problem.

17. To make your running life complete, finish at least one marathon.

18. Don't talk while running uphill. Let someone else carry the conversation.

19. **You can always run a little bit farther than you think possible.**

20. Don't be a whiner. Nobody likes a whiner, not even other whiners.

21. Treat your body with kindness and respect.

22. Drink skim milk.

23. Double knot your shoelaces before the start of a race.

24. Show appreciation to cheering spectators. Wave or give them the thumbs-up sign.

25. Remember that walking out the door is oftentimes the toughest part of a run.

26. Warm-up before running.

27. Cool-down after running.

28. Support sponsors who support road races and let them know why.

29. Don't let the very young run in very long races.

30. Don't run in strange cities without first asking if there are areas to be avoided.

31. Don't make excuses.

32. Keep a packed running bag in your car. Take advantage of unexpected opportunities to run.

33. Don't hide trophies. Display them.

34. Run as many of Runner's World's "top 65 races" as possible.

35. Don't make running your life. Make it part of your life.

36. During group training runs, don't let anyone run alone.

37. Run relaxed.

38. Use sunscreen.

39. Never run in black socks.

40. Be enthusiastic.

41. Remember that long runs are good opportunities for creative thinking.

42. Never trust a motorist to stop and look before turning right on red.

43. Keep promises, especially ones made to yourself.

44. Learn by listening to experienced runners.

45. Pace yourself in running and in life.

46. Drink several glasses of water a day, even more when racing in the heat.

47. Don't expect a small race to be like a big race and vice versa. Each size race has its pros and cons.

48. Don't skip ahead in finish line chutes. Maintain your correct position.

49. Buy new running shoes too soon rather than too late.

50. Let your doctor know you are a runner and how much running you do.

51. Find a running partner.

52. When doing group runs, start on time no matter who's missing.

53. Eat more pasta and less red meat.

54. Don't be strictly a weekend runner.

55. When you like the way a race is organized, say so in a letter to the editor of the local newspaper.

56. When you see ways to improve a race, write to the race director.

57. Never publicly predict how you'll do in a race.

58. Don't bring baby joggers and babies into adult races.

59. Never wear new running shoes for the first time in a race.

60. Keep a tube of Vaseline in your running bag.

61. Dedicate the important races you run to someone. Let that someone know in advance.

62. Never run in a plain white T-shirt.

63. Remember that "too busy" is not a good excuse for failing to run.

64. Listen to Nike and "Just Do It."

65. Just don't over do it.

66. Learn CPR.

67. Run defensively. Make eye contact with motorists.

68. **Stop worrying and go for a run. The problem will be there when you return, but it won't seem as bad.**

69. Remember that running friendships are like every other kind of friendship. Patience and understanding are required.

70. Keep toenails trimmed, but don't cut them the night before a race.

71. Stay for the awards ceremony even if you don't have a chance at a trophy.

72. Don't do anything strenuous the day before a race. Put your feet up.

73. In hot weather races take two cups of water at every aid station. Drink one and pour one on your head.

74. Think twice before buying the most expensive pair of running shoes in the store.

75. The faster you are the less you should talk about your times.

76. Better to start out too slow than too fast.

77. Save your running magazines.

78. Take running into consideration when planning vacations.

79. Keep a quarter in your pocket. One day you'll need to call for a ride.

80. Never run the entire 26.2 miles during marathon training. Limit your longest training runs to about 20 miles.

81. Buy a chest of drawers and use it strictly for your race T-shirts and running gear.

82. Store running shoes in an out of the way spot.

83. Never make critical comments about someone's weight, age or running speed.

84. The slower you are, the farther back you should line up at the starting line.

85. Don't buy running shoes if you can't stand the color.

86. If your favorite race sells commemorative posters, buy one. Have it framed.

87. Never be the last one to leave the post-race party.

88. The best way to learn about an unfamiliar place is to go for a run and explore.

89. Wear sandals when using public showers.

90. Have friends who will cheer for you at races.

91. Learn the history behind your favorite race.

92. Know the course of every race you run - before running it.

93. Don't clench your hands into fists while running. Relax.

94. Attend the pre-race pasta dinner.

95. Never take the elevator if there are stairs.

96. Have at least one running partner who is a member of the opposite sex.

97. Don't compare yourself with other runners.

98. Compete on an empty or near empty stomach and on an empty colon.

99. Never trust a strange dog.

100. **Remember that the marathon doesn't really start until the 20-mile mark.**

101. Pump your arms faster and your legs will follow suit.

102. Run in all seasons.

103. From time to time remind yourself of the advantages of being a runner.

104. Remember that all runners are equal, some are just faster than others.

105. Never run in a T-shirt that says anything offensive.

106. Buy your official race photograph.

107. Run hills. Hills build character.

108. Be supportive of beginning runners.

109. Run in races that support good causes.

110. Become the kind of runner others enjoy running with.

111. Don't eat strange food in strange restaurants the night before a race.

112. Keep a bottle of aspirin in the medicine chest and tray of ice cubes in the freezer.

113. Be patient when recovering from an injury.

114. Ignore people who are negative about running.

115. Don't ignore persistent pain.
See a doctor.

116. Attend a high school cross
country meet.

117. Carry identification when
running.

118. When running out of town
also carry the name of your hotel.

119. Every so often open your stride and run as fast as you can.

120. When running with friends, don't bring your dog or wear headphones.

121. Keep in mind that the later in the day it gets, the more likely it is that you won't run.

122. Own a good running watch. A good running watch doesn't have to be expensive.

123. Send notes of congratulations to finishers of marathons.

124. Wear reflective material when running at night.

125. Learn to jump rope, a good workout if the weather is too bad to run outside.

126. **Before running a marathon find someone who has done that race and ask them to talk about the experience.**

127. Applaud during award ceremonies.

128. Make sure at least one person is waiting for you at the end of a marathon.

129. When traveling by air, keep your running gear in a carry on.

130. There are rookies in every race. Be helpful.

131. For a change of pace, get driven out and then run back .

132. Stay at the official race hotel or as close to it as possible.

133. Find out where water is available on your running routes.

134. Remember that races don't usually have enough portable toilets. Plan accordingly.

135. Read the race application. All of it.

136. **Remember that if it was easy, everybody would be a runner.**

137. Never waste an opportunity to tell someone they ran a good race.

138. Follow hard running days with easy running days.

139. Run on Christmas morning.

140. To run fast in races, run fast in training.

141. To make a route seem shorter than it actually is, run it often.

142. Take deep breathes when standing nervously at starting lines.

143. If marathon training can't be a priority in your life, don't sign up to run one until it can be.

144. When standing at starting lines, remind yourself how fortunate you are to be there.

145. When you run out of gas, run on guts.

146. Keep a warmup suit in your car.

147. Remember that inside every runner beats the heart of a warrior.

148. Run to the beat of your own drum.

149. Rent the movie "Chariots of Fire."

150. Get an annual physical.

151. Pick up the pace when the finish line is in sight.

152. Develop a network of running friends who can provide advice and support.

153. Remember that getting out of shape is much easier than getting into shape.

154. Never confuse the terms "cross-training" and "cross-dressing."

155. When meeting new business associates find out if they run. Running can open doors.

156. In big races don't complain about the time it takes to get over the starting line. The race wouldn't be much fun if it was just you and a few others.

157. Remember that the best friends you'll ever find are to be found in the running world.

158. **Start every race with three goals:**

1. **To finish.**
2. **To finish in a realistic time.**
3. **To finish in a personal best time.**

159. Wear your good running shoes only when running.

160. Keep a sense of humor when running or when doing anything else.

161. Remember that a bad day of running still beats a good day at work.

162. Be positive. When someone asks about your running, tell them it's going great and getting better.

163. Talk like a runner. "Singlets" are worn on warm days. "Tank tops" are worn to the beach.

164. Put your name and address on a luggage tag and attach it to the outside of your running bag.

165. Save the safety pins given to you with bib numbers and attach the pins to your running bag. Sooner or later they will come in handy.

166. Think twice before criticizing a race volunteer. Then think again.

167. When in an unfamiliar city, check in with the local running club, a great source of information and instant friendship.

168. Don't talk about your running injuries. People, especially non-runners, don't want to hear about your sore knee or black toe.

169. Sex is OK the night before a marathon, assuming, of course, the other person is willing.

170. Don't stop running to pick up change. Bending over for a dime isn't worth pulling a muscle or breaking your rhythm.

171. Don't always run alone.

172. Don't always run with people.

173. Don't give up.

174. Buy running gear a tad too big rather than a tad too small.

175. Don't believe any running shoe salesperson who says, "They just need breaking in."

176. Own a good rain suit.

177. Don't believe anyone who says, "Don't worry, my dog doesn't bite."

178. **Make running 1,000 miles in a calendar year one of your goals.**

179. Approach running as if the quality of your life depended on it.

180. Encourage children to run, but don't force them.

181. Make it a point to meet Bill Rodgers.

182. Ditto for Frank Shorter.

183. Stretch

184. Write to your local newspaper and ask that more coverage be given to running and racing.

185. Read Hal Higdon's "On the Run From Dogs and People."

186. Be hesitant about believing spectators who say, "Just a mile to go." Usually it's longer.

187. Eat more fresh fruit.

188. If you get a medal or finisher's pin at the completion of a race, wear it for the rest of the day.

189. Never date a cigarette smoker.

190. Help cigarette smokers quit by turning them into runners.

191. When angry, go for a run.

192. Learn how to use the Internet and check it for information about races and to communicate with other runners.

193. Remember that running is supposed to be fun. If it isn't, you are doing something wrong.

194. Limit alcohol consumption the night before a race.

195. When running with friends, avoid conversations about politics, abortion or gun control.

196. Stick to brand name running shoes.

197. Join your company's running team.

198. If your company doesn't have a running team, start one.

199. **Rejoice if your employer understands the value of exercise and makes it possible for you to run during the lunch hour or at some other point during working hours.**

200. Remember that no matter how slow you run it is still faster than someone sitting on a couch.

201. Submit an article about your running experiences for publication.

202. Don't organize a road race if making money is your sole purpose. Races are expensive and time consuming to organize.

203. Keep in mind that the harder you run during training, the luckier you'll get during racing.

204. Encourage others to run, but keep in mind that running isn't for everyone.

205. Show up at the starting line. That's half the battle.

206. When it's hot, run on the shady side of the street.

207. Don't always run the same distance.

208. If someone needs help during a race, stop and provide it.

209. Use a treadmill or find a place to run inside when weather conditions are too poor to be outside. Be especially cautious when visibility is poor.

210. If you get bored with running, spend time with beginning runners. Their enthusiasm is contagious.

211. Before starting a long run, fill your mouth with water and empty your bladder.

212. Never tell a marathon runner, "I know how you feel," unless you've had occasion to run 26.2 miles.

213. Remember that races aren't just for those who can run fast.

214. Avoid getting your feet wet if the race is a long one.

215. If you want to know everything about the Boston Marathon, read Hal Higdon's "Boston: A Century of Running."

216. Never throw away a marathon T-shirt.

217. Remember there are no short cuts to running excellence.

218. **Keep your head up and your eyes forward. No matter how tired you are, don't look down at your shoes.**

219. Keep a few business cards in your running bag.

220. Learn first aid.

221. Don't worry about the time you spend running. It's time well spent.

222. To get inspired, watch the New York City Marathon or the Boston Marathon.

223. During a race, take water offered by kids even if you just had a drink.

224. Save old running shoes to wear when painting or working in the yard.

225. Don't worry if you have to walk a little during a marathon. No rule says you can't.

226. Remember the best runs sometimes come on days when you didn't feel like running.

227. Be modest after a race, especially if you have reason to brag.

228. If you say, "Let's run this race together," then you must stay with that person no matter how slow the pace.

229. Think twice before agreeing to run with someone during a race.

230. Smile when crossing finish lines.

231. Remember that there is nothing boring about running. There are, however, boring people who run.

232. Run through lawn sprinklers.

233. Look at hills as opportunities to pass people.

234. If winters are cold and snowy where you live, run a fall marathon instead of a spring marathon. Summer training is nicer than winter training.

235. Don't be pushed into doing races you don't want to do.

236. **If you aren't sweating, you aren't doing it right.**

237. Videotape your child's first race.

238. Make the most of your God given talent.

239. Remember that distance running is like cod liver oil. At first it makes you feel awful, then it makes you feel better.

240. When going out of town for a big race, splurge and get an expensive hotel room.

241. Never is it too late to become a runner.

242. Don't stop in a finish line chute. Keep walking.

243. Include a self addressed, stamped envelope when sending for race applications.

244. Shake hands with those standing around you at the starting line and wish them good luck.

245. Tell non-runners that the best time to start running is right now.

246. Ride a bike.

247. Don't let the pressures of work stop you from being a runner.

248. When tired, concentrate on your running form.

249. Present yourself with a nice gift after running a marathon.

250. The little shampoos and soaps from hotel rooms are perfect for your running bag.

251. Don't believe spectators who say, "You're looking good."

252. **Never throw away the instructions to your running watch.**

253. Never run through a cow field in a new pair of shoes.

254. Don't let the sight of a hill intimidate you. They usually aren't as bad as they look.

255. Don't go to bars to meet people. Find them in running clubs and at races.

256. Remember that good running habits are as hard to break as bad running habits.

257. Run through a golf course in the early morning.

258. Get your significant other involved with running.

259. Take a picture of someone in a race and send it to them.

260. Don't take marathons lightly. The experience can bring runners to tears, happy and sad.

261. Be conservative in the clothes you wear to work, but not in the clothes you wear for running.

262. Keep toilet tissue in your running bag.

263. Have a piece of running art in your home.

264. Ignore people who have reasons why you can't or shouldn't run a marathon.

265. Remember that most people who don't run are jealous of those who do run.

266. When it's hot, run where water is available.

267. To find out what you're made of, run a marathon.

268. Take a small, inexpensive camera to races.

269. Never miss an opportunity to run along the ocean.

270. Don't try to outrun dogs.

271. **Don't trust runners who show up at races claiming to be tired, out of shape or not feeling well. They get strong when the starter's gun goes off.**

272. Don't run races so slow that you cross the finish line feeling as if you could run miles more.

273. Participate in at least one run a year that raises money for a charity.

274. If you intend to run only one marathon in your life, make it one of the big ones.

275. Take inventory often. Is your running going in the direction you want?

276. Join a fitness club.

277. Most people are interested in hearing about the great race you ran. They are only interested once, however.

278. When it's hot, go out with the wind at your back. You'll enjoy having it in your face on the way back.

279. Seek variety in the routes you run.

280. Run Thanksgiving morning. You'll feel less guilty about what you do later in the day.

281. Listen to your body. It sends messages.

282. To clear the mind, go for a run.

283. Shorten your stride when it's slippery.

284. Don't run with a fever.

285. Keep in mind that sometimes it takes more discipline NOT to run
than it does TO run.

286. To help your body recover, run slow and short the day after a marathon.

287. Drink water before feeling thirsty.

288. Eliminate from your running vocabulary the words "try," "should" and "ought."

289. To get rid of a side stitch, slow down.

290. Take responsibility for your own health.

291. Don't skip breakfast.

292. Be sure you can run a distance before you race that distance.

293. Minimize salt intake.

294. Dress in layers.

295. Think positive.
Act positive.
Be positive.

296. Get to the starting line earlier than you think necessary. The bigger the race, the earlier that should be.

297. Don't wait for perfect weather. If you do, you won't run very often.

298. Know the early warning signs of heat-related illness, which include lightheadedness, dizziness, unsteadiness, headache, chills, goose bumps and nausea.

299. Respect the wind. The higher the breeze, the faster the heat loss.

300. Don't wait until there's time to run. Make time.

301. Be careful when running on indoor tracks. The tight turns and banked surface can cause injury.

302. Remember there are no losers in a race. There are only those who don't get to the finish line as quickly as the winner.

303. To race well, race often.

304. Make note of where the public bathrooms are in the area where you run.

305. Keep a roll of duct tape close at hand. If you are a race official, sooner or later that tape will save the day.

306. Applaud loudest for the runners out on the course the longest.

307. Remember that running changes people, almost always for the better.

308. Don't go to races without cash. There are usually things to buy.

309. When tempted to stop being a runner, make a list of the reasons you started.

310. Be aware that when a race course is billed as "challenging" it means "really tough."

311. Never use pain killing drugs as a way to run through an injury.

312. Never shake your fist or make any sort of gesture at someone driving a car, no matter how inconsiderate they were.

313. Be the most careful during the hottest part of the day.

314. There really is something called "second wind." Hang on until you get yours.

315. Yield to vehicles no matter who is supposed to have the right of way.

316. Never run alongside very old or very young racers. They get all the applause.

317. Road racing is not a team sport. You succeed on your own.

318. Run into sunsets.

319. Ditto for sunrises.

320. When going away on vacation, pack more running outfits and socks than you think you'll need.

321. Run through the French Quarter of New Orleans on a rainy morning.

322. Expect aches and pains. It happens to all runners.

323. Don't run immediately after eating.

324. Own a necktie with runners on it.

325. If you make a pact to run a race together, go across the finish line holding hands.

326. If the back side of the bib number has space for filling in your name, address and medical information, take a moment and write it down.

327. **Remember that without goals, training has no purpose.**

328. Don't try sport drinks for the first time during a race.

329. During training runs, let the slowest runner in the group set the pace.

330. Don't attempt a marathon in the first year or two of your running career.

331. Send a "good luck" note to someone attempting their first marathon.

332. Tell non-runners that the best time to start running was 20 years ago.
The second best time is today.

333. Go for broke, but be prepared to be broken.

334. Spend more time running on the roads than sitting on the couch.

335. Learn how to change into running clothes in an automobile.

336. Compliment runners on their achievements.

337. Before buying a house or renting an apartment consider what running will be like in that neighborhood.

338. Don't be embarrassed by the way you look running. It's the way you feel that counts.

339. Remember that "fun runs" have that name for a reason.

340. Keep your head in the clouds and your feet on the ground.

341. Have several running heroes, including the one you see in a mirror.

342. Be in Boston on Patriot's Day.

343. Never put wet running shoes close to a heater.

344. Don't run on your toes - unless, of course, you are a ballet dancer or a sprinter.

345. Don't spit into the wind or on the person running alongside.

346. If you've got a big race upcoming, forget the volleyball, softball, racquetball or any other sport that can increase your chances of injury.

347. Don't procrastinate when it comes to filling out race entry forms. You might not get a T-shirt. You might not even get into the race.

348. Remember that hard work pays off, especially in running.

349. Keep a log. Record every mile you run.

350. **Be patient with motorists who interrupt your run to ask for directions.**

351. Never give blood the day before a race.

352. Show respect for race officials.

353. To race in the heat,
train in the heat.

354. Don't wear running shoes
when participating in other
sports.

355. Visit Washington, D.C. and run on the mall connecting the Lincoln Memorial and the Capitol building.

356. Make progress in your training but progress at your own rate.

357. Courtesy counts in running, just as it does every place else in life.

358. Don't run if it's too hot.

359. Be realistic about your level of fitness.

360. Remember that "winning" means different things to different people.

361. Get behind someone when running into a headwind.

362. Be honest. Line up at starting lines where you belong.

363. Develop a finishing kick.

364. Don't start your finishing kick so soon that you have to slow down before the finishing line.

365. Don't talk about your running weaknesses.

366. Keep a fresh T-shirt in your running bag.

367. Avoid running through areas populated by dogs.

368. Don't feel guilty about taking a nap. Sometimes, especially when long distance training, naps are needed.

369. Remember that in the race for physical and mental fitness, there is no finish line.

370. Commit 100 percent to a marathon or forget it.

371. Wear out but don't rust out.

372. When someone asks how your running is going, tell them, "Great."

373. Before starting a race, know your goal. Finishing is a legitimate goal.

374. Be competitive if that's enjoyable. Avoid competition if it makes you uncomfortable. Running offers both choices.

375. Find a mentor.

376. Accept trophies and other running awards with a smile and a "thank you."

377. Be patient. It takes time to become the runner you want to be.

378. Act confident even if you aren't. Nobody will know the difference.

379. Unless you make your living as a runner, don't take running too seriously.

380. Never ridicule anyone's running, not even as a joke.

381. Know when not to run.

382. Don't run if it's lightning.

383. Don't be a bandit runner.

384. Never exaggerate your running accomplishments.

385. Don't tolerate bandit runners.

386. Don't get discouraged. Not every run will feel good. Not every race will be a personal best.

387. Remember that runners who never fail are runners who never try anything great.

388. Be friendly and helpful to anyone running their first race or first marathon.

389. Start a scrapbook for your race pictures, bib numbers, ribbons and other running memorabilia.

390. When racing, find someone who is running the pace you want to run. Let that pacer pull you along.

391. Slacken your jaw, run relaxed.

392. Use racing shoes only for racing.

393. Be a persistent runner.

394. Don't be a stubborn runner.

395. Don't make every race "do or die."

396. Don't be cocky. There is always someone faster.

397. Wear nice outfits when racing. It won't make you run faster but it will make you look better and feel better.

398. If you've been drinking alcohol, don't run, don't even walk.

399. Remember there are no bad runs. Some are just better than others.

400. During races remember that everyone is suffering with you.

401. To grow old gracefully, run gracefully.

402. Never ask someone if they plan on running another marathon until they've had time to forget what they went through during the previous one.

403. Remember that the most efficient pace is an even pace.

404. Don't buy cheap running shoes.

405. Think about running, but never think about it more than actually doing it.

406. Run today. Tomorrow it may not be possible.

407. Know your limits.

408. Never tell a runner that he or she doesn't look good in tights.

409. Get to bed earlier than usual for the two nights proceeding a marathon.

410. Don't feel guilty for not running today or for taking a few days off.

411. Don't give out tips on how to run the race course until you find out if the person you're talking with is in your age group.

412. Never lose your composure.

413. If your daily run starts feeling like torture, take a break. Try biking, swimming or long walks.

414. Never confuse the Ben-Gay tube with the toothpaste tube.

415. The most enjoyable runs can sometimes come on days when you least expect it.

416. Never ask someone why their running has gotten slower.

417. Learn how to drink water on the run.

418. If you can't drink while running, try using a straw. If that doesn't work, stop and drink.

419. Don't run a marathon because others want you to. Run a marathon only if you want to.

420. Use running for internal benefits, not external rewards.

421. Leave the car home now and then. Walk to work.

422. Remember that the longer you sit and think about running the harder it is to get up and actually do it.

423. Always remember that heat and humidity are the enemy.

424. Remember that sweat never hurt anybody.

425. Treat wheelchair athletes the same as every other runner.

426. To find heroes go to a marathon and watch the middle and back of the back runners cross the finish line.

427. When talking with novice runners, remember what it was like when you first started running.

428. **At every race give at least one person words of encouragement.**

429. To save energy on long runs, listen more than you talk.

430. Once a year run the mile as fast as you can. Record the time.

431. There is such a thing as a runner's high, although not all runners are fortunate enough to experience it.

432. Talk to your family doctor before starting marathon training.

433. Never be too proud to stop running and walk home, but don't make it a habit.

434. Never apologize for doing the best you can.

435. Remember that preventing running injuries is easier than curing them.

436. Run with successful people. Success rubs off.

437. Hug people after races.

438. Visualize yourself crossing the finish line, arms raised in triumph.

439. The better you know a race course the smarter and faster you'll run it.

440. Remember that running cures fatigue.

441. Force yourself to hold back during the early miles of a marathon.

442. Before deciding to run a marathon, make sure your family supports the idea.

443. Never get in a line at a portable toilet if there's less than five minutes until the start of the race. That's why God invented bushes.

444. Remember that to be a runner is to be above average.

445. Reduce your mileage when tapering for a race or when recovering from a race.

446. To learn about someone, run a long distance with them.

447. Run across the Golden Gate Bridge.

448. Ditto for the Brooklyn Bridge.

449. Have a copy of "The Runner's Repair Manual" by Dr. Murray Weisenfeld in your home library.

450. To lose weight, run more and eat less. Be sure to eat healthy.

451. Don't worry about running in races with the fastest runners in the world. Just make sure none of them are behind you at the start.

452. In severe weather make a point of telling someone your route and when you expect to return.

453. Remember that winning trophies oftentimes has to do with who shows up.

454. Change "I'm not a good runner" to "I'm getting better and better.

455. Do one long run a week, keeping in mind that "long" means different things to different people.

456. Say a prayer before the start of a race. Include everyone in the race in your prayer.

457. Don't try to explain a runner's high. Just enjoy it.

458. Not drinking enough water is the easiest way for a runner to get into trouble.

459. Don't try anything new the day before a race or during a race.

460. Wear the socks you run in when trying on new running shoes.

461. Remember that pain is God's way of saying something is wrong.

462. Read "Personal Best" by George Sheehan.

463. Don't race too often.

464. Be humble in victory.

465. Be brave in defeat.

466. Be cheerful all the time.

467. Don't bounce while stretching.

468. Treat yourself to a massage after running a marathon.

469. Marry someone who runs or, at the very least, someone who understands why you do.

470. Think twice before organizing a new race. There are already more than 15,000 in the United States.

471. Running is simple. Don't make it complicated.

472. When upset or angry, go for a run.

473. Remember that there will be good running days and bad running days, and there's no predicting which day will happen when.

474. Don't let your breathing get out of control.

475. Celebrate your birthday by going for a longer than usual run.

476. Learn to cross country ski, and do that when the weather is too bad to run.

477. Don't hang around with people who smoke.

478. Have someone videotape your favorite race.

479. Don't interfere with traffic by running in the middle of the road.

480. Buy a combination lock and keep it with your running bag.

481. Don't overstretch. Too much of a good thing can be a bad thing.

482. Pay attention to your running form, especially when tired.

483. Don't get nervous before the start of a race. Unless you are a professional, you are there to enjoy yourself.

484. Don't start a race unless you intend to finish it.

485. Wave to oncoming runners.

486. Remember that running is always enjoyable. Sometimes, though, the joy doesn't come until the end of the run.

487. Recognize when you've done your best and when you haven't.

488. Remember that sad times are good times to run.

489. When traveling, check the local newspaper, call the YMCA or check with a running store to see if a race is scheduled. Race T-shirts make great souvenirs.

490. Remember that the first year in a new age group offers the best opportunity for trophies.

491. Celebrate your personal running victories.

492. Get enough sleep.

493. Be wary about running in first ever races. They haven't had time to work out the kinks.

494. Remember that motivation is the key to success in running as it is in every sport.

495. If you run on a team or belong to a club, have a group picture taken every year.

496. Once a year, run in a race you've never participated in before.

497. Stay limber, something that becomes increasingly important as you celebrate birthdays.

498. Improve your self-esteem. Run a marathon.

499. If you believe you'll never run a marathon, you won't.

500. Remember there is no such thing as an easy race.

501. Read this book again. It is impossible to remember 500 things after just one reading.